SPORTS and Recreation

Serena and Venus WILLIAMS
Tennis Stars

by Gregory N. Peters

CAPSTONE PRESS
a capstone imprint

Trailblazers Books are published by Capstone Press,
1710 Roe Crest Drive, North Mankato, Minnesota 56003
www.capstonepub.com

Library of Congress Cataloging-in-Publication Data
Peters, Gregory N.
Serena and Venus Williams tennis stars / by Gregory N. Peters.
pages cm. — (Trailblazers. Sports and recreation)
Includes bibliographical references and index.
Summary: "Describes the lives of tennis stars Serena and Venus Williams
from birth to becoming champions"— Provided by publisher.
ISBN 978-1-4765-8075-3 (library binding)
1. Williams, Serena, 1981- —Juvenile literature. 2. Williams, Venus,
1980- —Juvenile literature. 3. Women tennis players—United States—
Biography—Juvenile literature. 4. African American women tennis
players—Biography—Juvenile literature. I. Title.
GV994.W49P48 2014
796.3420922—dc2   2013030381

Editorial Credits
Christine Peterson, editor; Gene Bentdahl, designer; Eric Gohl, media
researcher; Eric Manske, production specialist

Photo Credits
Corbis: Brian Smith, 14, Colorsport/4044-5, 17, Dallas Morning News/Vernon
Bryant, 42 (bottom), Duomo, 34, EPA/Gerry Penny, 41, EPA/John G. Mabanglo,
39, Xinhua Press/Yin Gang, 27; Dreamstime: Zair1952, cover; Getty Images:
Allsport/Al Bello, 12, Allsport/Ken Levine, 6; Newscom: Abaca/Gouhier-
Hahn-Nebinger, 30, AFP/Carol Newsom, 22, AFP/Greg Wood, 24, Atticus
Images/Paul Harris, 9, 10, EPA/Andy Rain, 33, Fotosports International,
18, Getty Images/AFP/Simon Maina, 42 (top), UPI Photo Service/Christine
Chew, 28, ZUMA Press/Brian Peterson, 32, ZUMA Press/Globe Photos, 21;
Shutterstock: Featureflash, 37, Phil Anthony, 4

Printed in China by Nordica.
1013/CA21301911
029013   007739NORDS14

TABLE OF CONTENTS

Venus and Serena
Williams in 1999

CHAPTER 1

Young Champions

The two young women walked onto the tennis **court**. They began to warm up. One woman threw a tennis ball high in the air. The woman swung her **racket**. Thwack! The ball sailed over the net.

The women looked alike, yet they were different. One woman was very tall. Her body was **lean**. Her legs were long. The other woman was all muscle. She had powerful arms and legs.

Then the tennis **match** began. Both women hit the ball hard. They were strong. They were tough. They were fast. Yet **spectators** were not sure each woman really wanted to win. These women could beat anyone. Yet it was hard to beat each other. Why? They were sisters.

court – the surface on which tennis is played

racket – equipment used to hit a tennis ball

lean – having little or no fat

match – the best of three or five sets of tennis

spectator – a person who watches an event

Venus talks to her dad on the tennis court in 1990.

Venus Williams was born June 17, 1980. Her sister Serena was born September 26, 1981. Their parents are Richard and Oracene Williams. Venus and Serena have three older sisters.

The Williams family lived in Compton, California. Compton was a rough place. There were gangs there. There was a lot of crime.

Richard played tennis. He taught Oracene how to play too. Richard wanted Venus and Serena to be tennis stars. He gave Venus a tennis racket. She was only 4 years old.

Venus loved playing tennis with her dad. She was good at it. She thought tennis was fun. She also liked spending time with her dad. Later Serena felt the same way. Their mom played tennis with them too. She was a tough **coach**.

It was hard to play tennis in Compton. The courts were cracked. Gangs hung around. Richard told the girls to stay safe. If they heard gunshots, they had to drop to the ground.

coach - the person who trains an athlete or team

Venus and Serena became very good.
They played against other girls. They played in
tournaments. Venus and Serena were tough and
strong. They beat every girl they played.

Richard and Oracene wanted the girls to be
good at tennis. They also wanted them to do well
in school. They made sure the girls studied.
School came first. Tennis was second.

The Williams family also wanted Venus and
Serena to be proud. Some people were mean to
them because they were African-Americans.
The girls heard **racist** shouts when they played.
They ignored the cruel words. They answered with
great tennis.

In 1991 the Williams family moved to Florida.
Rick Macci became the girls' coach. The girls went
to Macci's tennis academy. Macci was their coach
until 1995. Then Richard became their coach again.

tournament – a contest in which the winner is the one who
wins the most games or matches

racist – treating people cruelly or unfairly because of their
race or skin color

Venus practices in
Compton, California,
with her father.

Serena (left) and Venus practice together.

CHAPTER 2

Sibling Rivalry

Venus and Serena trained together. Richard Williams was a tough coach. Richard said the girls did not need to play against other girls. They could play against each other. That was the best **competition**.

Many people did not like Richard. They thought he was too proud. They said he wanted the girls to be tennis stars so that he could be famous. Richard ignored the mean words. He knew he was a good father. He and Oracene made sure Venus and Serena had love and **discipline**.

Richard and Oracene were very proud of their girls. They told everyone how good the girls were. They believed their girls would be the best tennis players in the world.

competition – a contest between two or more people
discipline – having self-control

11

Venus played her first professional game in 1994.

The Williams sisters had busy lives. They went to
school. Good grades were important to them. They
also had to play tennis. The girls practiced for hours.
The sisters hit ball after ball. They learned how to
hit powerful **serves**. The girls practiced hard.
They got better and better.

Finally it was time to become **professional** tennis players. Venus turned pro on October 31, 1994. She was 14 years old. Venus' first professional game was fantastic. She hit powerful **volleys**. She slammed the ball over the net again and again. Venus won the match. Serena loved watching her sister play. She thought it was thrilling.

Next Venus faced a player from the country of Spain. Venus played hard, but she lost the match.

serve - the first hit in a tennis match

professional - a person who makes money doing something other people do for fun

volley - a shot made by hitting the ball across the net before it bounces on the ground

Venus kept playing. She practiced all the time. She and Serena played against each other. Their parents kept teaching them. They only let the girls enter a few tournaments each year. They did not want the girls to get bored with tennis. They wanted the girls to stay strong and happy.

Serena turned pro in September 1995. She was 13. Her father told reporters Serena was better than Venus. Serena could not wait to play. She wanted to prove she could be a great player.

Serena lost her first professional match. She was not happy. Serena knew she had not played well. Still, she did not get **discouraged**.

Richard and Oracene were proud of their daughters. But Oracene worried about them. She did not want them to turn pro so young. Oracene wanted them to wait until they were 16. She and Richard didn't let them play in many tournaments.

Serena (bottom left) and Venus (top middle) with their parents

discouraged – having lost belief in oneself

Venus and Serena have a lot in common. They both have big, strong serves. Venus and Serena send the ball booming over the net. Both girls are fast runners. They race all over the court. The girls hit back almost every ball that is hit to them.

These sisters are also **aggressive**. They hit the ball hard. Both girls work hard to make every shot. They never hold back. These sisters never play it safe.

Venus and Serena are a lot alike. But they are also different. Venus is tall. She is lean and slim. Serena is more **muscular**. She is not as tall. Serena gets more excited than Venus when they play. She often yells or grunts. You always know how Serena feels.

aggressive - strong and forceful

muscular - having many muscles

Venus (left) and Serena (right) work hard on the court.

Fastest Serve

Venus holds the record for the fastest serve ever hit by a woman. The speed was 130 miles (209 kilometers) per hour. Guess who has the second fastest serve? Serena. She hit a serve at 129 miles (208 km) per hour!

The All England Club in Wimbledon, London, England, is the home of the Wimbledon Championships.

CHAPTER 3

Grand Slams

Imagine a big tennis match. You sit in the stands along with thousands of people. Everyone cheers as two players walk onto the court. Both players are really good. They are **champions**. You can't wait to watch them play.

Tennis players compete in matches all over the world. But nothing is as exciting as a **Grand Slam** match. Grand Slam tournaments are the biggest matches in a tennis player's career. Only the best players can win a Grand Slam.

Four Grand Slam tournaments are played every year. The Australian Open is played in Melbourne, Australia. The French Open is played in Paris, France. Wimbledon is played in London, England. The U.S. Open is played in Queens, New York.

champion - a winner of a competition
Grand Slam - one of the four major tennis tournaments in a year

Both Venus and Serena have done well at Grand Slams. Serena was the first of the sisters to win a Grand Slam. She won her first Grand Slam at the U.S. Open in 1999. Venus won her first Grand Slam at Wimbledon in 2000. She won her second Grand Slam at the U.S. Open just a few months later.

Both Venus and Serena have defeated other champions. Each one has earned Grand Slam titles. However, they faced their toughest **challenge** when they played each other. The sisters feel **bittersweet** about playing against each other. Playing each other makes them happy. It also makes them sad, because one of them has to lose. When Venus defeated Serena at the Australian Open in 1998, she told her sister she was sorry.

challenge – something difficult that requires extra work
bittersweet – happy and sad at the same time

Serena celebrates her win at the 1999 U.S. Open.

Venus (left) and Serena hug at the net following their
2001 U.S. Open match.

By 2001 Venus and Serena had played against each other many times. Both were champions. But they had never faced each other in a Grand Slam championship. That day finally came in September during the U.S. Open final. It was the first time two sisters faced each other in the **final** in more than 100 years.

The **stadium** was packed. More than 23,000 fans were there. They cheered and yelled for the sisters. The match lasted just over one hour. Both Venus and Serena hit the ball hard. At first Serena was stronger. She sent the ball back over the net with every volley. Then Venus took over. She hit the ball so hard that it knocked Serena's racket right out of her hand.

In the end Venus won. The two sisters met at the net. They hugged. "I love you," Venus told Serena.

final - the last match in a tennis competition

stadium - a large building in which sports events are held

Serena shows off photos from her four "Serena Slam" wins of 2002 and 2003.

Over the years Venus and Serena have faced each other in eight Grand Slam finals. Serena has won six times.

Serena also achieved something amazing in 2002. She did not play in the Australian Open that January. Serena had injured her ankle. She was ready to play in the French Open in June. Serena beat Venus in the finals. Then she defeated Venus to win the Wimbledon title. Next was the U.S. Open. Serena won again and beat her sister. In January 2003, Serena defeated Venus and won the Australian Open. She held all four Grand Slam titles at the same time.

Serena won four straight Grand Slam events in two different years. Her achievement could not be called a Grand Slam. So it is called the "Serena Slam."

Better Together

Venus and Serena are great players by themselves. What happens when they team up? They are almost unbeatable.

When one tennis player plays one other player, it is called a **singles** match. A **doubles** match is when two players play against two other players. Venus and Serena's sister act is perfect on the doubles court. The sisters have played in 13 Grand Slam doubles finals. They won all 13 titles.

One of the most exciting doubles matches happened at Wimbledon in 2012. Serena won the singles title. Later that same day, she and Venus played in the doubles final. Serena and Venus beat their **opponents**. "I couldn't have done it without her," Venus said.

Serena was happy to play with her sister. "In singles, it's OK if I let myself down, but I don't want to let her down."

Venus (left) and Serena compete in the women's doubles final at the 2012 Wimbledon Championships.

singles – a tennis match played by one person on each side

doubles – a tennis match played by two people on each side

opponent – the person competing against another player

Serena and Venus wave to the crowd after their doubles victory at the 2000 Olympic Games in Sydney, Australia.

CHAPTER 4

Golden Victories

On September 15, 2000, hundreds of **athletes** marched into the Olympic stadium in Sydney, Australia. Among them were Venus and Serena. The sisters were playing in their first **Olympic Games**. The sisters were proud to represent the United States. They smiled and waved to the crowd.

Venus won the singles gold medal. Serena did not win a singles medal. But would she go home empty-handed? Fans watched the doubles match to see what would happen.

Venus and Serena struck gold again. The sisters won the gold medals in doubles. Both women smiled proudly as they stood on the medal stand. The American flag was raised. It was a proud moment for the Williams sisters.

athlete – a person who plays a sport
Olympic Games – a competition of many sports events held every four years

Venus goes for a shot during a match at the 2008 Olympic Games in Beijing, China.

In 2004 Venus and Serena competed in the Olympics in Athens, Greece. This time they did not win any gold medals. That changed in 2008. That year the Olympics were in Beijing, China. The sisters won gold medals again as doubles partners. Together they could not be beaten.

The next Olympics was held in London, England, in 2012. By then both Venus and Serena were more than 30 years old. Many tennis players quit playing before they reach that age. Could Serena and Venus still win? The world waited to see.

Serena at the 2012 Olympic Games in London.

At last the moment arrived. The sisters were in London for the 2012 Olympics. They had both come a long way. They started as little girls playing tennis on the broken courts of Compton. Now they were in London, looking for gold. Both women had battled injuries. They had both suffered serious medical problems. Now they faced young players who were great and wanted to win. The crowds waited to see what the Williams sisters would do.

Battling Illness

Most athletes get hurt during their careers. This has happened to both Venus and Serena. They have played with **sprained** ankles and torn muscles. They have also faced major illness. In 2011 Venus had to withdraw from the U.S. Open. She had a disease that makes people feel tired. It can cause a lot of pain. Serena has had health problems too. In March 2011, she had suffered a blood clot in her lung. Both sisters took time off to get better. Venus and Serena did not let illness keep them down for long.

Venus did not make the finals of the singles matches. But Serena did. She won the gold medal in singles. Venus was proud of her sister. However, the sisters were not done winning medals.

Once again Venus and Serena were partners in the doubles finals. Once again they won. The sisters came home with the doubles gold medals. Each one of them had four Olympic gold medals.

Serena and Venus celebrate their win at the 2012 Olympic Games in London, England.

sprain – an injury to a joint or muscle caused by twisting or straining

CHAPTER 5

Beyond the Court

Venus and Serena are great tennis players. They also studied hard in school. They wanted to be champions in life. They wanted to know more than just how to hit a ball over a net.

Both Venus and Serena love clothes. They often wear bright, daring clothes on the tennis court. Before the Williams sisters came along, most women tennis players wore white. Not Venus and Serena. Serena once wore bright pink on the court. At the 2002 U.S. Open, she wore a stretchy black outfit. The girls' clothes changed the way other players dressed. Serena and Venus have fun showing flair with their outfits.

Serena wore a daring outfit at the 2002 U.S. Open.

Venus and Serena know how to dress. They know how to **design** too. Venus has a **degree** in fashion design. In 2007 she started a fashion line named EleVen. Venus also owns an **interior** design firm called V Starr Interiors.

In 2004 Serena started her own clothing line. She named it Aneres which is "Serena" spelled backward. In 2009 Serena started a collection of handbags and jewelry called the Signature Statement. Serena is not shy about her talent. "I'm an unbelievable designer," she wrote. "I was born to be a designer. I worked hard to be a tennis player. I don't work hard to be a designer."

Venus and Serena are also writers. In 2010 Venus published a best-selling book, called *Come to Win*. Serena also wrote a book. *On the Line*, her autobiography, was published in 2009.

design - to make a plan for how to make or build something

degree - a title given to a person for finishing college courses

interior - the inside of something, especially a building

Serena (left) and
Venus on the red
carpet in 2005.

Back on the court, Venus and Serena believe in fairness for everyone.

Both athletes have faced **racism**. They have been called terrible names just because they are African-American. One well-known incident happened at a tournament at Indian Wells, California, in 2001. The sisters and their father were booed. Richard said he heard people saying racist things. Venus and Serena refused to play at Indian Wells ever again.

The Women's Tennis **Association** (WTA) makes the rules for pro players. This group says players have to play at Indian Wells. If they don't, they have to pay a **fine** . Serena and Venus don't care. They want to stand up for themselves and others, even if they have to pay a fine.

The BNP Paribas Open is played in Indian Wells, California, where Venus and Serena were booed by the crowd.

racism - the belief that one race is better than others

association - a group

fine - a fee for breaking the rules

Venus and Serena also want female tennis players to be treated fairly. Some tournaments used to pay men more than they pay women. Venus and Serena fought to change that. In 2005 Venus met with **officials** from the French Open. She complained that the French Open did not pay women as much as men. The French Open did not change its **policy**.

Venus had better luck at Wimbledon. This tournament also did not pay women as much as men. In 2006 Venus wrote an essay saying that Wimbledon's rule was wrong. The British government agreed. They asked Wimbledon to change. In 2007 it paid female champions the same as men.

The French Open soon changed its policy too. Venus Williams was proud and happy. She became the first woman to benefit from the changes.

---

official - a person of power who makes decisions

policy - a plan to help people make decisions

Venus holding the 2007 Wimbledon trophy

Titles and Medals

Serena believes in helping others too. She takes part in many sports **clinics**. These clinics are held at schools and community centers. Serena plays with children at these clinics. She teaches them how to play tennis. She gives them a dream.

Children in Africa are close to Serena's heart. In 2008 she helped pay for a school in Matooni, Kenya. It is called the Serena Williams Secondary School. This school helps children get an education.

Venus and Serena Williams changed the game of tennis forever. They are strong, powerful role models. They have built good lives for themselves. Venus and Serena are true champions.

clinic – a class that teaches a sport to a group

Major Championships Won by Venus and Serena Williams

Venus Williams:

Grand Slam Singles Titles:
Wimbledon: 2000, 2001, 2005, 2007, 2008
U.S. Open: 2000, 2001

Grand Slam Doubles:
Australian Open: 2001, 2003, 2009, 2010
French Open: 1999, 2010
Wimbledon: 2000, 2002, 2008, 2009, 2012
U.S. Open: 1999, 2009

Olympic Games:
gold medal, singles: 2000
gold medal, doubles: 2000, 2008, 2012

Serena Williams:

Grand Slam Singles Titles:
Australian Open: 2003, 2005, 2007,
    2009, 2010
French Open: 2002
Wimbledon: 2002, 2003, 2009, 2010, 2012
U.S. Open: 1999, 2002, 2008, 2012, 2013

Grand Slam Doubles Titles:
Australian Open: 2001, 2003, 2009, 2010
French Open: 1999, 2010
Wimbledon: 2000, 2002, 2008, 2009, 2012
U.S. Open: 1999, 2009

Olympic Games:
gold medal, doubles: 2000, 2008, 2012
gold medal, singles: 2012

Read More

Bailey, Diane. *Venus and Serena Williams: Tennis Champions.* Sports Families. New York: Rosen Central, 2010.

Donaldson, Madeline. *Venus & Serena Williams.* Amazing Athletes. Minneapolis: Lerner Publications Co., 2011.

Sandler, Michael. *Tennis: Victory for Venus Williams.* Upsets & Comebacks. New York: Bearport Pub., 2006.

Bibliography

Page 23 • from an interview with CNN *Sports Illustrated* (http://sportsillustrated.cnn.com/tennis/2001/us_open/news/2001/09/08/usopen_women_ap/).

Page 27 • from an interview with Tennis Guru (http://www.tennisguru.net/2012/07/venus-serena-williams-win-13th-grand-slam-doubles-title/).

Page 37 • from an interview with Associated Press (http://www.foxnews.com/story/0,2933,138502,00.html).

Internet Sites

FactHound offers a safe, fun way to find Internet sites related to this book. All of the sites on FactHound have been researched by our staff.

Here's all you do:
Visit *www.facthound.com*
Type in this code: 9781476580753

 Check out projects, games and lots more at **www.capstonekids.com**

Titles in this set:

The Best of College Basketball

Muhammad Ali Boxing Legend

The Negro Leagues

Serena and Venus Williams Tennis Stars

Glossary

academy (uh-KAD-uh-mee) • a school that teaches special subjects

aggressive (uh-GREH-siv) • strong and forceful

association (uh-so-see-AY-shuhn) • a group

athlete (ATH-leet) • a person who plays a sport

autobiography (aw-tuh-by-AH-gruh-fee) • the story of a person's own life written by that person

bittersweet (BIT-er-sweet) • happy and sad at the same time

challenge (CHAL-uhnj) • something difficult that requires extra work

champion (CHAM-pee-uhn) • a winner

clinic (KLIN-ik) • a class that teaches a sport to a group

coach (KOHCH) • the person who trains an athlete or team

competition (kahm-puh-TI-shuhn) • a contest between two or more people

court (KORT) • the surface on which tennis is played

defeat (di-FEET) • to beat someone in a competition

degree (di-GREE) • a title given to a person for finishing college courses

design (di-ZYN) • to make a plan for how to make or build something

discipline (DISS-uh-plin) • having self-control

discouraged (diss-KUR-ijd) • having lost belief in oneself

doubles (DUH-buhls) • a tennis match played by two people on each side

final (FYE-nuhl) • last match in a competition

flair (FLAIR) • natural skill or ability

Grand Slam (GRAND SLAM) • one of the four major annual tennis tournaments: the Australian Open, the French Open, the U.S. Open, and Wimbledon

inspire (in-SPIRE) • to influence and encourage people in a good way

interior (in-TIHR-ee-ur) • the inside of something, especially a building

lean (LEEN) • having little or no fat

match (MATCH) • a game or series of games

muscular (MUHS-kyuh-ler) • having well-developed muscles

official (uh-FISH-uhl) • a person of power who makes decisions

Olympic Games (OH-lim-pick GAYMS) • a competition of many sports events held every four years in a different country; people from around the world compete against each other

opponent (uh-POH-nuhnt) • a person who competes against another player

policy (POL-uh-see) • a plan to help people make decisions

professional (pruh-FESH-uh-nuhl) • a person who makes money doing something other people do for fun

racism (RAY-si-zuhm) • the belief that one race is better than others

racist (RAY-sist) • treating people cruelly or unfairly because of their race or skin color

racket (RAK-it) • a stringed frame with a handle used in tennis

serve (SURV) • the first hit, aimed at the other team's side of the net

singles (SING-uhls) • a tennis match played by one person on each side of the net

spectator (SPEK-tay-tur) • a person who watches an event

sprain (SPRAYN) • an injury to a joint or muscle caused by twisting or straining

stadium (STAY-dee-um) • a large building in which sports events are held

tournament (TUR-nuh-muhnt) • a contest in which the winner is the one who wins the most games or matches

volley (VOL-ee) • a shot made by hitting the ball over the net before it bounces on the ground

Index